Editor   Karen Barker
Language Consultant   Betty Root
Natural History Consultant   Dr Gerald Legg

Carolyn Scrace is a graduate of Brighton College of Art in England, specializing in design and illustration. She has worked in animation, advertising and children's fiction and non-fiction. She is a major contributor to the popular *Worldwise* series and *The X-ray Picture Book* series, particularly **Amazing Animals**, **Your Body**, and **Dinosaurs**.

Betty Root was the Director of the Reading and Language Information Center at the University of Reading in England for over twenty years. She has worked on numerous children's books, both fiction and non-fiction.

Dr Gerald Legg holds a doctorate in zoology from Manchester University in England. His current position is biologist at the Booth Museum of Natural History in Brighton, England.

David Salariya was born in Dundee, Scotland, where he studied illustration and printmaking, concentrating on book design in his post graduate year. He has designed and created many new series of children's books.

An SBC Book conceived, edited and designed by
The Salariya Book Company
25 Marlborough Place, Brighton BN1 1UB

First published in Great Britain in 1999 by Franklin W[...]

First American edition 2000 Franklin Watts/Children's [...]
A Division of Grolier Publishing
90 Sherman Turnpike
Danbury, CT 06816

Visit Franklin Watts/Children's Press on the Internet at:
http://publishing.grolier.com

Library of Congress Cataloging-in-Publication Data

Scrace, Carolyn.
        The journey of a whale / written and illustrated b[...]
Carolyn Scrace; created & designed by David Salariya[...]
        p.   cm. --- (Lifecycles)
        Includes index.
        ISBN 0-531-14521-2 (lib. bdg)
        ISBN 0-531-15420-3 (pbk)
        1. Gray whale--Migration--Juvenile literature.
I. Salariya,
David. II. Title. III. Series.
QL737.C425S37 1999
599.5'221568--dc21   98-26[...]
                                                      C[...]

The Journey of a Whale

Written and Illustrated by Carolyn Scrace

Created & Designed by David Salariya

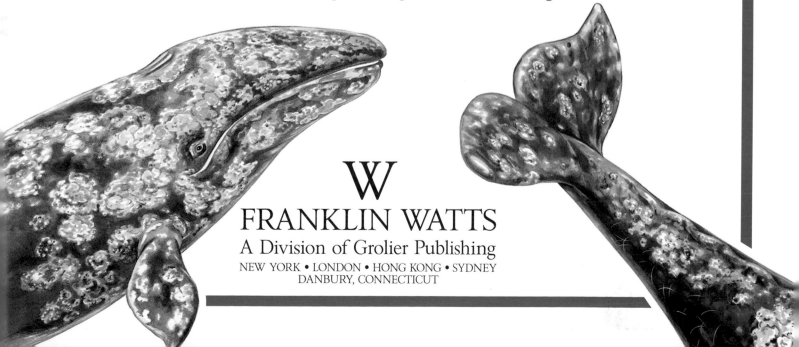

W
FRANKLIN WATTS
A Division of Grolier Publishing
NEW YORK • LONDON • HONG KONG • SYDNEY
DANBURY, CONNECTICUT

Whales are mammals that live in the sea. Their home is in the Arctic and Antarctic oceans (see map on page 26), where there is plenty of food.

In the fall, the polar oceans become icy. Then the whales swim to warmer waters in order to mate.

When spring comes the whales return home to the polar oceans. Their whole journey is called a *migration*.

In this book you can follow the amazing migration of a gray whale.

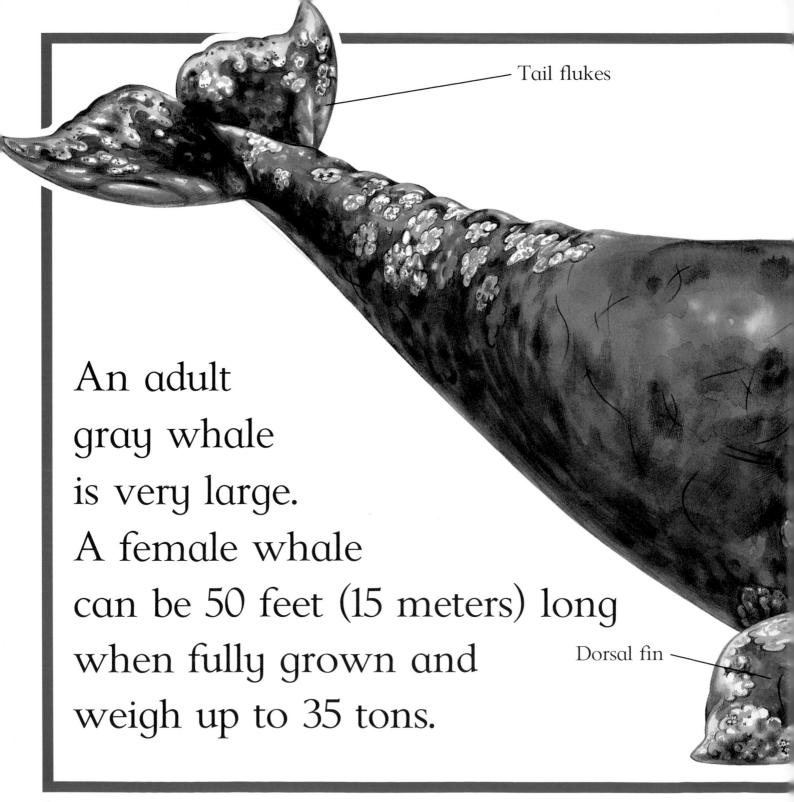

Tail flukes

An adult
gray whale
is very large.
A female whale
can be 50 feet (15 meters) long
when fully grown and
weigh up to 35 tons.

Dorsal fin

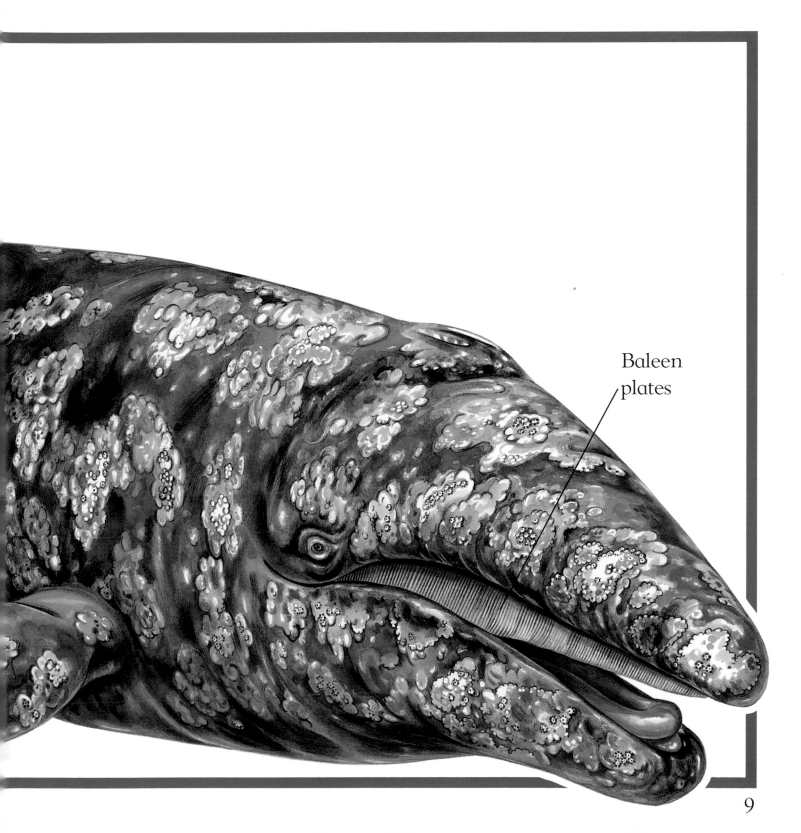

Baleen
plates

Some whales have teeth
and can eat fish.
The gray whale
has no teeth.
It eats small
animals called
krill which float
in the sea.

Krill

In the summer, gray whales
live in the Arctic Ocean.
There is plenty of krill to eat.
The whales spend the long
summer days feeding.

When fall comes, whales start swimming toward warmer seas. It is winter by the time they reach the warm water. Now the male and female whales mate. The female whales become pregnant.

Male whales spray huge jets of water from their blowholes.

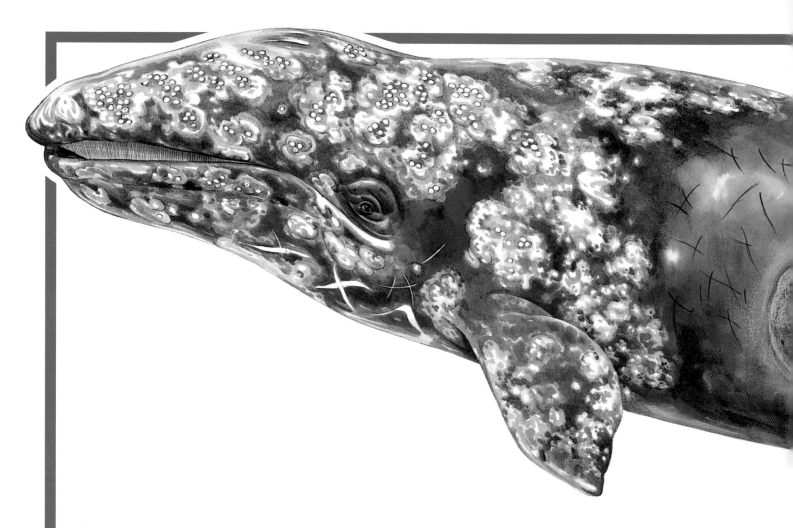

In spring, the whales start
their return journey.
They swim thousands of miles
back to the cool polar oceans.

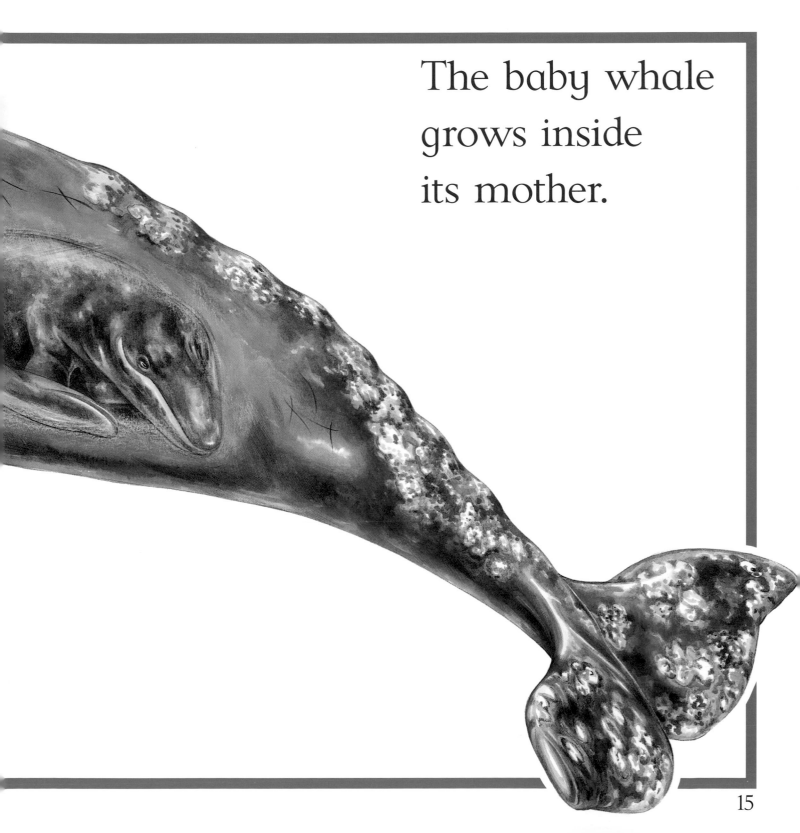

The baby whale
grows inside
its mother.

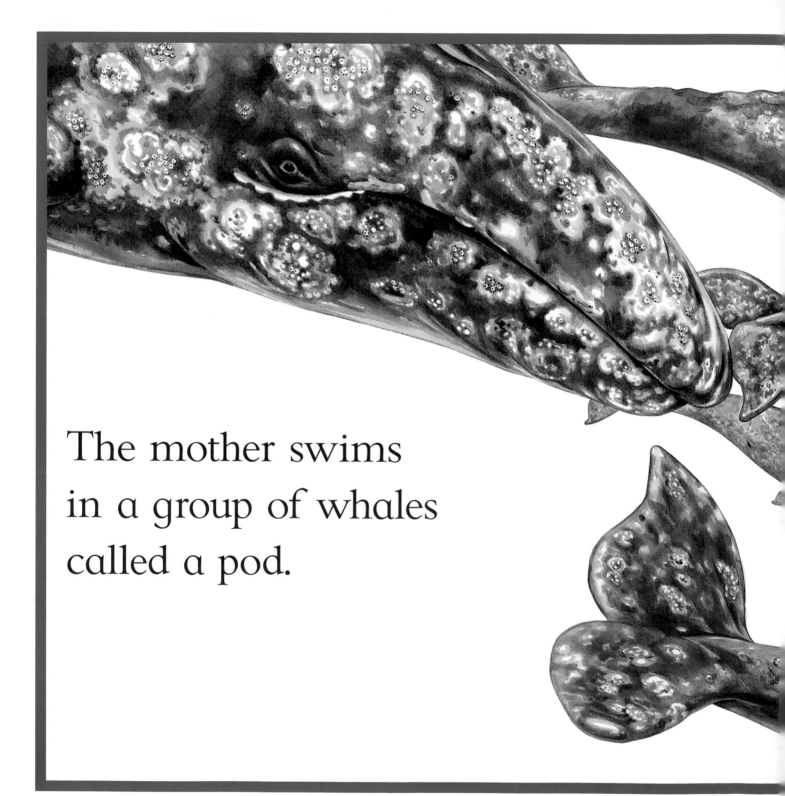

The mother swims
in a group of whales
called a pod.

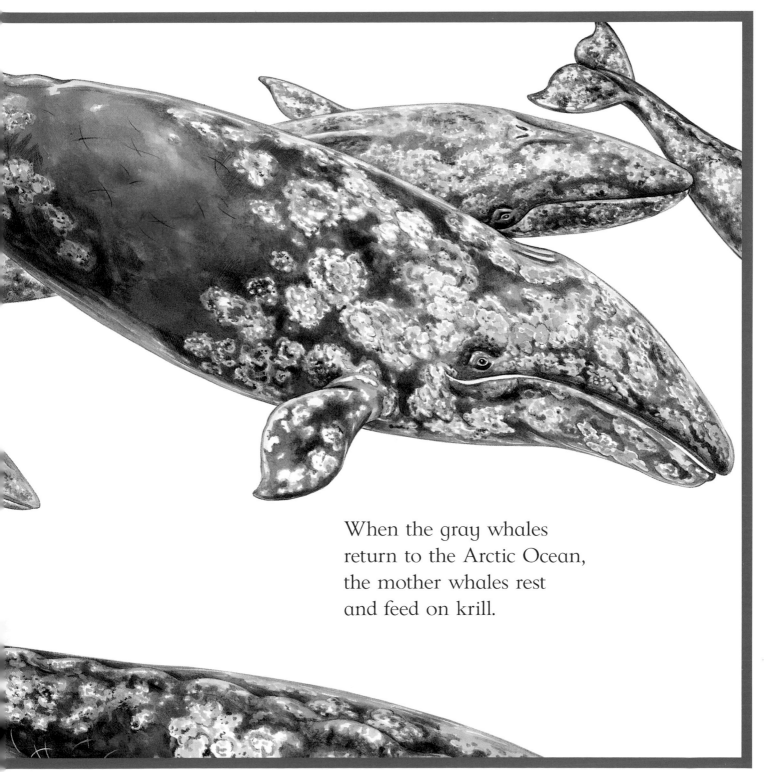

When the gray whales
return to the Arctic Ocean,
the mother whales rest
and feed on krill.

A baby whale takes one year
to grow inside its mother.

Fall comes again,
and the whales start
their migration.
By winter, they have
reached warmer seas.

The baby whale
is ready to be born.

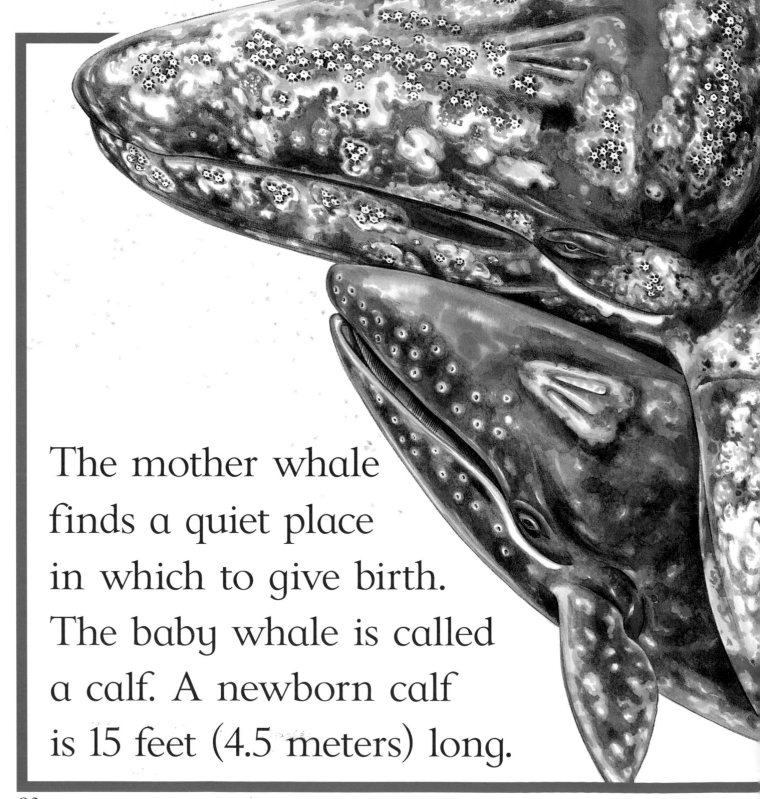

The mother whale
finds a quiet place
in which to give birth.
The baby whale is called
a calf. A newborn calf
is 15 feet (4.5 meters) long.

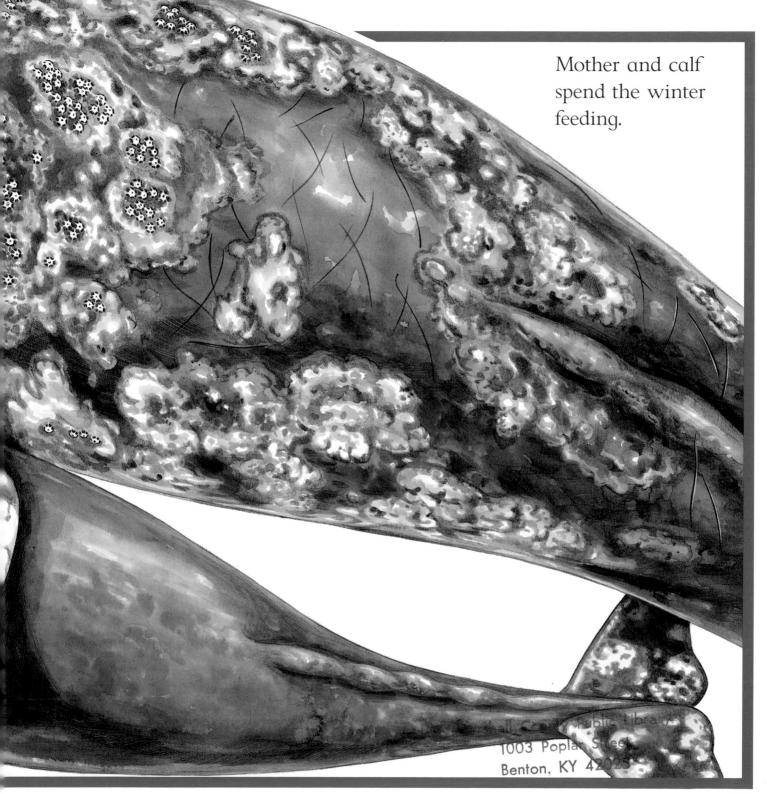

Mother and calf spend the winter feeding.

21

When spring comes,
the mother and calf start
to swim home.
It takes them many months
to get back to the polar oceans.
The calf must grow a thick
layer of fat, or blubber, to keep
it warm.

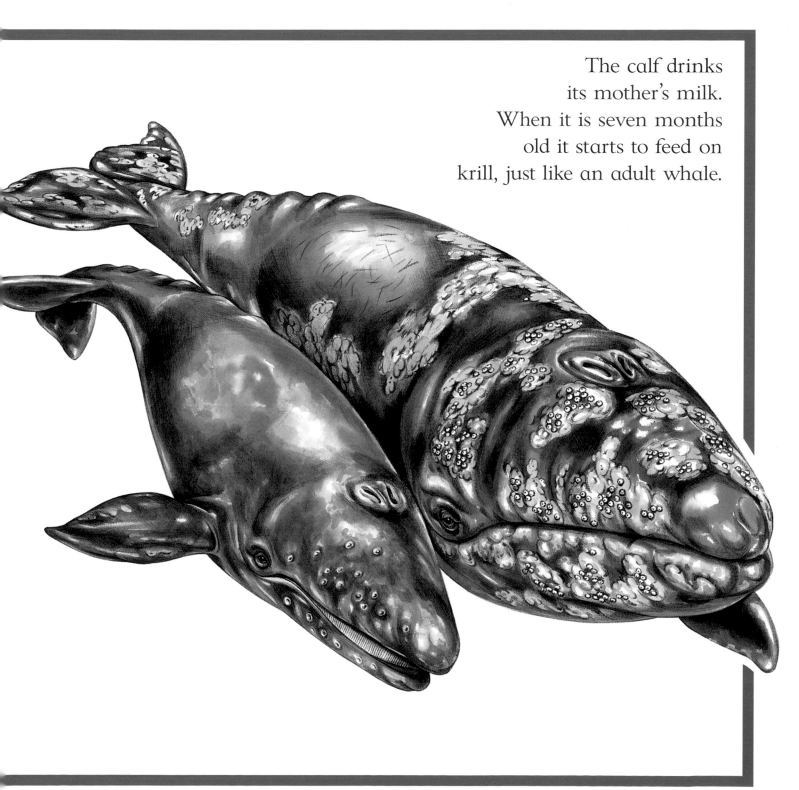

The calf drinks
its mother's milk.
When it is seven months
old it starts to feed on
krill, just like an adult whale.

By summer, the whales and their young are home.

They have finished their migration.

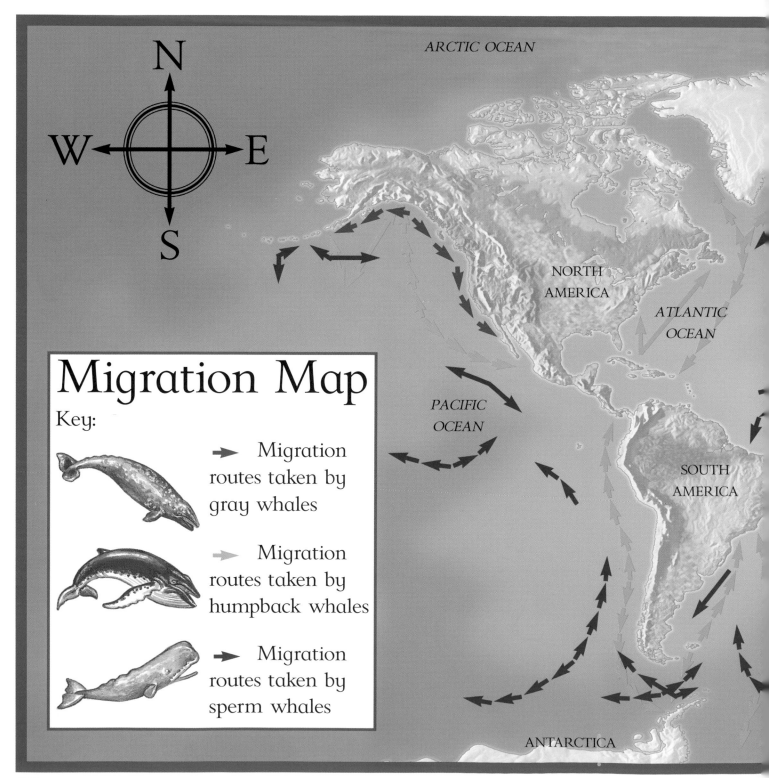

Migration Map

Key:

- Migration routes taken by gray whales
- Migration routes taken by humpback whales
- Migration routes taken by sperm whales

ARCTIC OCEAN

NORTH AMERICA

ATLANTIC OCEAN

PACIFIC OCEAN

SOUTH AMERICA

ANTARCTICA

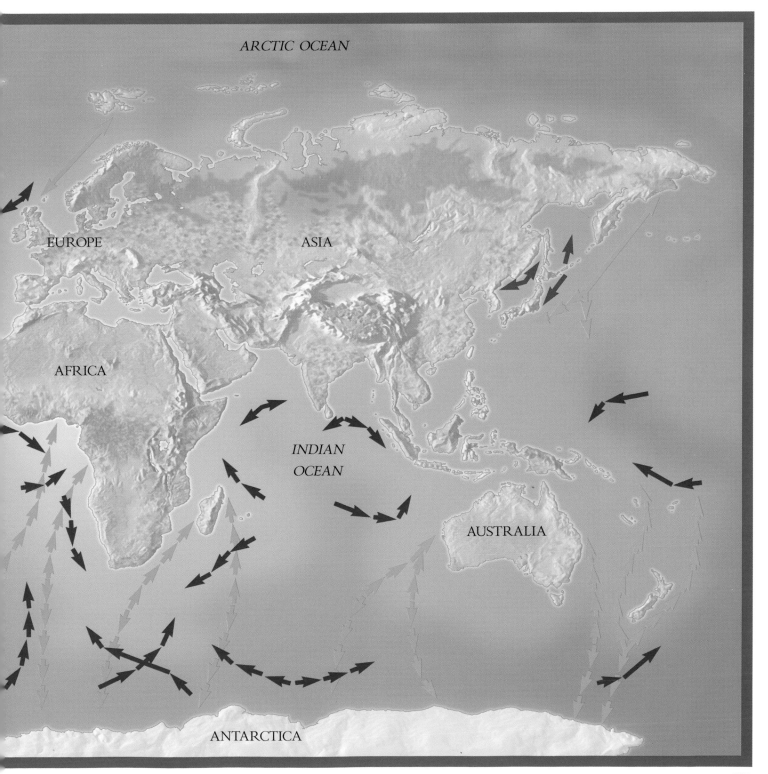

ARCTIC OCEAN

EUROPE

ASIA

AFRICA

INDIAN
OCEAN

AUSTRALIA

ANTARCTICA

27

Whale Words

Antarctic Ocean
The ocean around the south pole

Arctic Ocean
The ocean around the north pole

Baleen plates
The sieve-like parts of a gray whale's mouth. When a gray whale takes a gulp of sea water it uses the baleen plates to filter the water for food

Blowhole
The pair of nostrils that gray whales have on the tops of their heads

Calf
A baby whale

Dorsal fin
The triangular shaped fin on the back of a whale

Krill
Tiny shrimp-like animals that live in the sea

Mammal
Warm-blooded animals, usually with backbones

Mate
When male and female whales join together. It is how a baby whale is made

Pod
A group of whales

Polar
Anything at or near the north or south poles. For example, polar bears live near the north pole

Pregnant
Carrying an unborn baby inside the body

Tail flukes
The wide, flat end of a whale's tail. They help the whale to move through the water

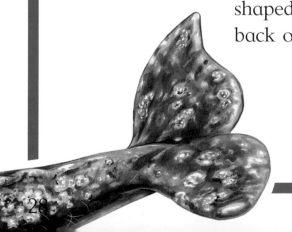

Index